Young Cornrows Callin Out the Moon

Poem by Ruth Forman

Illustrations by Cbabi Bayoc

Children's Book Press   San Francisco, California

frontyard neither

when the sun go down

5

we don have no backyard
no sof grass rainbow kites mushrooms butterflies

6

we got South Philly summer
when the sun go down

cool after lemonade n black eye peas
full after ham hocks n hot pepper greens
corn bread coolin on the stove

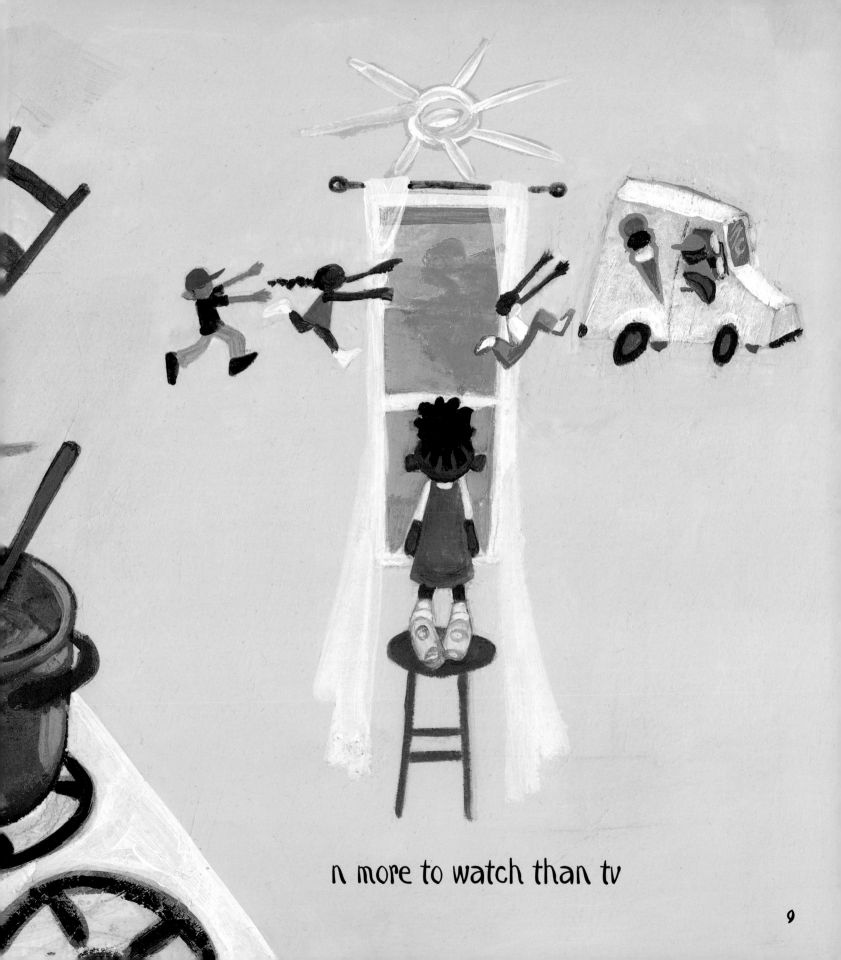

n more to watch than tv

we got double dutch n freeze tag n kickball
so many place to hide n seek n

look who here Punchinella Punchinella
look who here Punchinella inna zoo

11

13

we got the corner store
red cream pop
red nails Rick James the Bump the Rock

n we know all the cheers

we got pretty lips
we got callous feet healthy thighs n ashy knees
we got fine brothers we r fine sistas
n
we got attitude

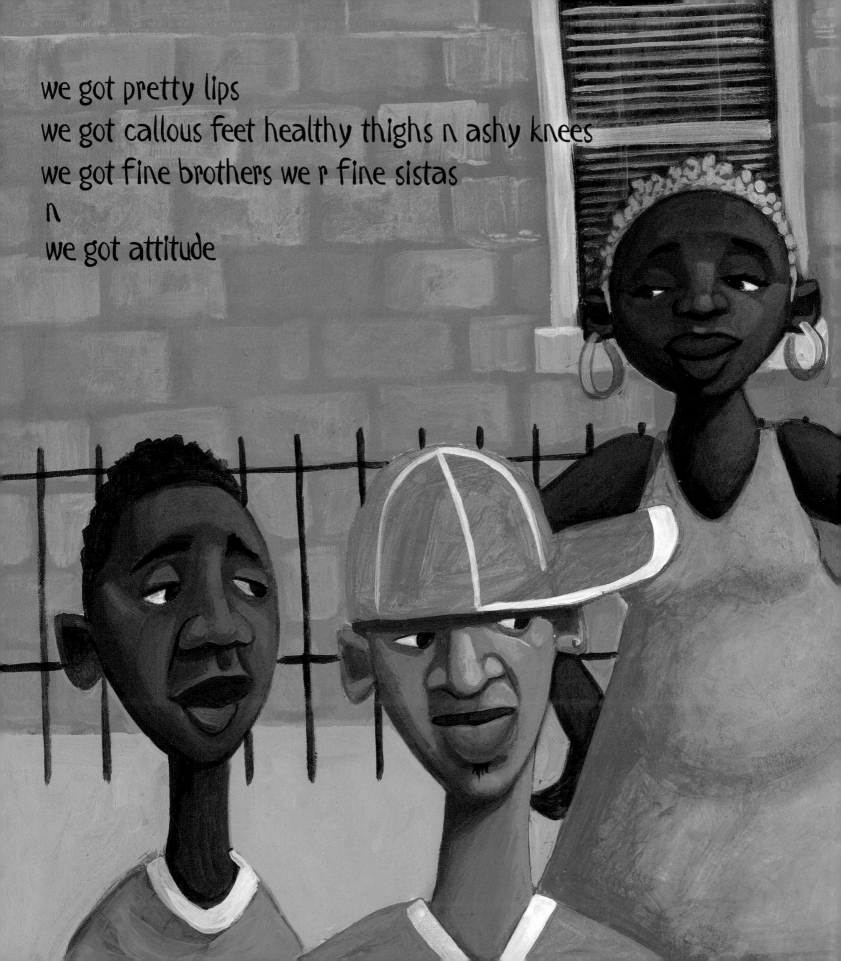

we hold mamma knees when she snap the naps out
we got gramma tell her not to pull so hard

we got sooo clean cornrows when she finish
n corn bread cool on the stove

so you know

we don really want no backyard
frontyard neither

wit black magic n brownstone steps

23

I spent many a summer in Philadelphia on the brownstone steps of my aunts and uncles. *Young Cornrows Callin Out the Moon* is a celebration of those summers, when I played outside until after the streetlights came on among cousins, friends, knees, cornrows, jump rope, games, the ice cream truck, laughter, and dance. The concrete landscape was a summer song I kept in my pocket long after the August moon left for September.

I use poetry to capture and convey how something feels. I use images, movement, smells, tastes, sounds, textures, and rhythm, so that people who hear or read my poetry can experience a certain feeling. I hope with this poem you can step inside those South Philly summers.

What do you love? What brings you joy? Can you describe it with images, smells, sounds, tastes, how something feels to the touch, or how people speak? Can you be really specific? Why not try a poem?

— *Ruth Forman*

Library of Congress Cataloging-in-Publication Data

Forman, Ruth.
  Young cornrows callin out the moon: poem by Ruth Forman; illustrations by Cbabi Bayoc.
    p. cm.
  ISBN-13: 978-0-89239-218-6
  ISBN-10: 0-89239-218-5
  1. African American girls–Juvenile poetry. 2. Summer–Juvenile poetry. 3. South Philadelphia (Philadelphia, Pa.)–Juvenile poetry. 4. Children's poetry, American. I. Bayoc, Cbabi, ill. II. Title.
  PS3556.O7334Y68 2007
  811'.54–dc22   2006020447

Young Cornrows Callin Out the Moon first appeared in Ruth Forman's collection of poems entitled *We Are the Young Magicians*, published by Beacon Press in 1993.

photo by Christine Bennett

Ruth Forman is a prize-winning poet, author, and friend of words. She likes to think magic dwells in the pen, if only we let it out. She still loves to sit on brownstone steps and her favorite time is summer dusk, right after dinner, when the air is still warm and indigo gently kisses us into the night. She lives in Los Angeles.

For Uncle Jr., our big, beautiful Forman family, and all the young cornrows callin out the moon. — RF

Editor: Dana Goldberg
Design & Production: Carl Angel
Production Coordinator: Janine Macbeth
Special thanks to Melanie Chan, Jamal Cooks, Jeremiah Jeffries, Alexandre Petrakis, José Ramírez, and the staff of Children's Book Press.

Quantity discounts available through the publisher for educational and nonprofit use. Distributed to the book trade by Publishers Group West.

Children's Book Press is a nonprofit publisher of quality multicultural literature for children. For a catalog, write: Children's Book Press, 2211 Mission Street, San Francisco, CA 94110. Visit our website: www.childrensbookpress.org

Printed in Singapore through Tien Wah Press
10 9 8 7 6 5 4 3 2 1

photo by Reine Bayoc

Cbabi Bayoc is a fine artist and illustrator whose work reflects his love of music and family. His paintings can be found in galleries and homes around the world, on album covers, in music videos, and on the pages of magazines and newspapers. He lives in St. Louis with his wife and children.

Dedicated to my own special cornrows: Reine, Jurni, Ajani and Birago..........SHMILY! – CB

FREE